There are more than 100 different species of ducks, which include swans and geese.

Baby ducks are called ducklings, adult men are called drakes, and adult women are called hens.

 **is for an African Goose.**

African geese aren't actually from Africa; they are domestic (meaning a farm animal) who came from wild swan geese.

My First Book about the Alphabet of Ducks

Amazing Animal Books
Children's Picture Books

By Molly Davidson

Mendon Cottage Books

JD-Biz Publishing

A is also for an Anas Platyrhynchos, the scientific name for a Mallard.

Mallards are dabbling ducks which means they eat mostly food found on the top of the water.

Only the men have bright green head feathers, the women are all brown and speckled.

 is for a Barrow's Goldeneye.

Barrow's goldeneye ducks live in northern Canada and Iceland.

Mother ducks will return to the same nest to lay their eggs year after year.

C is for a Canadian Goose.

Canadian geese are known to be very noisy and aggressive.

They migrate from northern Canada to the southern United States every year.

They fly in a V shape.

C is also for a Cygnus, the scientific name for a swan.

Swans are one of the largest flying birds, weighing up to 33 pounds and having a wingspan of up to 10 feet.

They live for about 10 years in the wild.

D is for a Domestic Duck.

Domestic ducks are raised by farmers for meat, eggs, and their fluffy warm down feathers.

They are harder to raise than chickens, so their meat and eggs are more expensive to buy.

They mainly eat slugs and insects.

 is for an Egyptian Goose.

Egyptian geese were considered sacred to the ancient Egyptians, who used them in much of their art.

They can be very mean if they feel their territory is threatened, they even fight in the air.

 **is for a Freckled Duck.**

Benjamint444 © <u>Wikimedia Commons</u>

A freckled duck is one of the rarest ducks in the World and is only found in Australia.

Mothers will sometimes lay their eggs in another ducks nest, so she doesn't have to use any energy in raising the ducklings.

They live in swamps in groups of up to 100.

G is for a Greylag Goose.

Greylag geese have been owned by farmers for almost 3,500 years!

They live in central Europe and Asia.

Ducklings will stay with their mother for a year, until her next brood of eggs hatch.

 **is for a Hooded Merganser.**

Hooded merganser boys are black and white and the girls are brown and tan.

Both boys and girls have a head crest that they can raise and lower.

They live in small ponds and lakes in North America.

I is for an Indian Runner Duck.

Indian runner ducks stand up tall and do not waddle but run around.

The girls can lay up to 200 eggs per year.

 **is for a King Eider.**

King eider ducks live in along the northern arctic coasts.

To find food they dive down into the sea water to find small plankton and other ocean insects.

Instead of quaking they make a choo-ooing sound.

L is for a Loon.

Loons swim with their bellies under the water.

Their feet make them excellent swimmers, but they are not able to walk on land very well.

M is for a Mandarin Duck.

Mandarin ducks are a dabbling duck found in East Asia and Western Europe.

Koreans believe these ducks represent peace, and complete love for your spouse and children.

M is also for a Muscovy Duck.

Muscovy ducks live in Mexico, and Central and South America.

The boys weigh about 15 pounds, but the girls only weigh about half as much, 6 1/2 pounds.

All Muscovy ducks have sharp claws on their feet and wide flat tails.

 **is for a Northern Pintail.**

Northern pintails can be found almost everywhere north of the equator.

They are very good swimmers and super fast flyers, because they fly with their wings behind them instead of to the side like other ducks.

O

is for an Oxyura Australis, the scientific name for a Blue Billed Duck.

Valorix © <u>Wikimedia Commons</u>

Blue billed ducks live in the wetlands of Australia.

They find food by scooping up mud from the bottom of ponds, then sifting out all the rocks and non food stuff.

P is for a Pilgrim Goose.

Pilgrim geese are owned by many farmers in Europe, Australia, and the United States.

During the American Great Depression is when this goose began to be bred, not by pilgrims settling the colonies from England.

is for a Ring-Necked Duck.

Ring-necked ducks live in lakes and ponds in North America.

They are a diving duck, and search the pond bottoms for snails, worms, and insects to eat.

They have a dark red ring around their necks, which may be hard to see, they are also called a ringbill.

 **is for Snow Geese.**

Snow geese spend their summers in Alaska, northern Canada, and Siberia.

They migrate south to Texas and Mexico in the winter.

They travel in groups of thousands of birds.

S is also for a Smew.

Fossils have been found that are very similar to a smew that are over 13 million years old.

Smew are a small bird, they are about 1 1/2 feet long.

They are a diving duck and eat mostly fish.

T is for a Teal.

There are many subspecies of a teal duck.

All the boys have brightly colored head feathers, and the girls are brown and tan.

The boys make a loud, noisy whistling sound.

U is for an Upland Goose.

Upland geese, also called Magellan geese, live on the southern tip of South America.

The boys are mostly all white and the girls are brown with black-striped wings.

 is for a Velvet Scoter.

Velvet scoter ducks live all over northern Asia and Europe.

They make their nests close to the sea, where they lay 7 - 9 eggs.

Like most ducks, their eggs take about one month to hatch.

 **is for a Whistling Duck.**

There are 8 different species of the whistling duck and they all live in tropical areas.

Whistling ducks have long legs and necks.

They make loud whistling calls to communicate.

Y is for Yellow-Billed Duck.

Yellow-billed ducks live in south eastern Asia and do not migrate.

They live in large, loud groups.

They lay 6 - 12 eggs in a nest build on the ground near the water.

Conclusion

I hope you have enjoyed reading about some amazing ducks.

One more fact, most ducks have two layers of feathers, a soft downy under layer for warmth, and an oily waterproof outer layer.

Our books are available at

1. Amazon.com

2. Barnes and Noble

3. Itunes

4. Kobo

5. Smashwords

6. Google Play Books

Download Free Books!
http://MendonCottageBooks.com

Publisher

JD-Biz Corp

P O Box 374

Mendon, Utah 84325

http://www.jd-biz.com/

www.ingramcontent.com/pod-product-compliance
Lightning Source LLC
Chambersburg PA
CBHW050902290526
45792CB00002B/671